Attracting and motivating new learners with ICT

Jackie Essom

promoting adult learning

ⓝiace

©2006 National Institute of Adult Continuing Education
(England and Wales)
21 De Montfort Street
Leicester
LE1 7GE

Company registration no. 2603322
Charity registration no. 1002775

NIACE has a broad remit to promote lifelong learning opportunities
for adults. NIACE works to develop increased participation in
education and training, particularly for those who do not have easy
access because of class, gender, age, race, language and culture,
learning difficulties or disabilities, or insufficient financial resources.

You can find NIACE online at **www.niace.org.uk**

Cataloguing in Publication Data
A CIP record of this title is available from the British Library

Designed and typeset by Book Production Services, London

Printed and bound in the UK by Latimer Trend
ISBN: 1 86201 276 8
      978 1 86201 276 9

Contents

Acknowledgements

NIACE would like to acknowledge the support of the Department for Education and Skills, without which this guide would not have been produced.

Thanks also go to Peter Lavender, Alan Clarke and Alastair Clark of NIACE for their helpful comments and suggestions, and to all the organisations that kindly provided case studies and examples of good practice in attracting and motivating new learners for this publication.

1

Introduction

Until now, basic skills have referred to literacy and numeracy. In today's society we believe it is as important that everybody can also use information and communications technology (ICT), particularly in the workplace. So we shall offer basic ICT skills as a third area of adult basic skills alongside literacy and numeracy within our Skills for Life programme.

21st Century Skills: Realising our Potential (DfES 2003)

What is ICT Skill for Life?

In the government's 2003 White Paper, *21st Century Skills: Realising our Potential*, information and communications technology (ICT) was acknowledged as a new skill for life, along with existing 'skills for life' – literacy, language and numeracy.

The Skills for Life Survey

The government's *Skills for Life* strategy is intended to help equip people with some of the essential skills they will need to function in today's competitive world – to make progress in their work and in society as a whole. The *Skills for Life Survey*, commissioned by the Department for Education and Skills, was conducted between June 2002 and May 2003. The survey covered adults aged 16–65 in England and aimed to produce a national profile of adult literacy, numeracy, ESOL (English for speakers of other languages) and information and communications technology (ICT) skills over five broad levels of competence: Entry Levels 1–3 and Levels 1 and 2.

Key findings of the survey

General education

On the whole, the survey found that those in employment had a higher level of literacy and numeracy skills than those who were not in employment, and that good skills in both areas tended to be associated with good wages.

However, a fifth of those interviewed (22 per cent) had no educational qualifications at all. This was as high as 40 per cent of those aged over 55. The *Skills for Life Survey* makes the point that

> *Low levels of literacy and numeracy can lead to social exclusion, denying people the opportunity to get the most out of what is available to the rest of society.*
>
> *Skills for Life Survey* (DfES 2003)

ICT

Findings from the survey showed that 10 per cent of those interviewed had a computer at home and 25 per cent used a home computer daily, mainly for word processing and for accessing the Internet and e-mail. The survey also found that, of those interviewed:

> 38 per cent used computers for education/learning, and
> 52 per cent had received some kind of formal training or education with computers.

However, the survey also highlighted that

> 15 per cent of those interviewed had never used a computer;
> younger people tended to be more frequent users of computers, and therefore had stronger ICT skills;
> only 36 per cent of 55–65 year olds were frequent users of computers, and more than one third of this age group (37 per cent) had never used one;

> those with learning difficulties limiting their activities in some way tended to perform at a much lower level in the survey's ICT assessments;

> those entirely outside the labour market tended to have much weaker skills;

> men tended to perform better than women;

> those who lived in areas of high deprivation were much less likely to be frequent users of computers.

We can see from these survey results how people with good literacy and numeracy skills *and* good ICT skills can usually expect to have more employment opportunities and better paid work, while those who don't may find themselves being socially excluded.

Respondents with good ICT skills tended to earn more money than those with less good ICT skills.

Skills for Life Survey (DfES 2003)

Over the last decade, ICT has become a more prominent sought-after skill. A large percentage of jobs now require some level of ICT skills – even those not traditionally associated with computers. For instance:

> Cleaners may need ICT skills to complete and submit their time cards online.

> Hairdressers now keep track of their clientele by keeping online records of their hair treatments, and also use online calendars to book appointments.

> Fitness instructors produce their own posters to advertise their classes.

> Doctors often type and print out prescription forms themselves – a big change from the days when prescriptions were handwritten and virtually illegible!

> Pharmacists now type and print out labels for medication.

We could all probably think of many other such examples. As a result, ICT is now being regarded as a new *basic skill* or *life skill*, along with literacy, numeracy and ESOL.

Increasingly, therefore, people who lack one or more of these basic skills are at an ever greater risk of becoming socially excluded.

Widening participation

For these reasons, much work is currently under way to improve the participation of learners from socially and economically disadvantaged groups in ICT-related activities. ICT has the potential to overcome many of the barriers faced by such groups in accessing education and training – but this assumes that they have access to ICT in the first place, are competent users of ICT, and have access to high-quality learning materials and good support systems.

Many groups in society feel themselves to be excluded from educational opportunities for a variety of reasons, which we will examine in the section on **'Barriers'** (page 16).

How can those who regard education with indifference (or even fear) be tempted back into learning? What can educators do to widen participation by making learning opportunities available to *all* adults?

The following sections of this guide take a look at these groups, the barriers they face and the strategies that educators can use to reach them. We will consider projects and initiatives that use ICT to deliver learning opportunities to many different groups, especially those that traditionally have been under-represented in educational provision.

The government's *Skills for Life* strategy identifies ICT as a means of delivering literacy, language and numeracy, as well as for embedding ICT skills within all other learning. Examples are contained within the guide.

We hope that this guide will provide organisers with some new ideas to consider when planning courses, and that tutors/trainers will be encouraged to incorporate ICT into their teaching/training sessions.

2

Engaging hard-to-reach learners

Who do we want to reach?

We are talking about people who are at a high risk of being socially and economically disadvantaged in our society today. A comprehensive list of groups that traditionally have been under-represented in educational provision was published in the Kennedy Report *Learning Works*, published in 1997 by the Further Education Funding Council. Such groups include:

> long-term unemployed people;
> older people;
> people with no or very low qualifications;
> people with low levels of literacy and/or numeracy;
> lone parents;
> ex-offenders and those on probation;
> some minority ethnic groups;
> travellers;
> refugees and asylum seekers;
> people with disabilities or learning difficulties;
> people with mental health difficulties;
> people with drug or alcohol dependency or those recovering from dependency.

You may have come across other groups that may be at risk of social exclusion because of the problems and barriers they face.

Barriers

So what are these barriers?

The most common barriers that socially excluded adults encounter are usually those associated with:

> age;
> health;
> disability;
> language;
> low self-esteem;
> lack of confidence.

Other major barriers face people living in disadvantaged areas of the country with few facilities such as childcare, and an unreliable and infrequent public transport system. Even when such services are available, their costs may be prohibitive to many on low incomes. There may be very limited learning opportunities available, particularly in rural areas.

For many, especially those with negative memories of their school days, there is also the fear of entering a formal educational institution. They may not have undertaken formal learning courses since they left school and may feel that learning is not for them or that they are too old to learn. The 2005 NIACE survey on adult participation in learning shows that over one third of adults (35 per cent) say they have not participated in any learning since leaving full-time education (Aldridge and Tuckett 2005).

How can they be reached?

Once we have identified the disadvantaged groups in our local communities, we need to think how best to reach out to members of these groups, engage them in learning and motivate them to continue. Let's look at some of the main points that should be taken into consideration.

Accessibility and flexibility

Learning needs to be flexible and designed to fit around people's work and life commitments. For instance, people such as shift workers, those with health problems, the homeless and parents of young children find it difficult to attend classes on an intensive or regular basis.

Points to consider

The following is an example of a further education centre that offers flexible learning opportunities and times to fit in with their learners' lives.

Brooksby Melton College in Melton Mowbray, Leicestershire, has established a 'Learning Shop' which offers free and flexible computer training to students of all ages. Classes in a variety of computer applications are on offer, and learners have the option of gaining recognised qualifications: they can study either for a 'Certificate in Using Information Technology' (Level 1) or for the higher level 'Diploma in Using Information Technology' (Level 2). The centre is open 56 hours a week, Monday to Saturday, enabling students to attend classes at a time to suit themselves and their personal circumstances. The only commitment is that they must attend the centre for 4–6 hours each week.

	Yes	No
Does your organisation provide crèche facilities where parents can leave their children while attending learning sessions?	☐	☐
Do you provide classes in the evenings or on Saturdays to fit in with your prospective learners' working lives?	☐	☐
How accessible are your premises for disabled people? Do you provide pictorial signs for those people who may have poor literacy or literacy difficulties? From October 2004, under the terms of the Disability Discrimination Act learning providers must make reasonable adjustments to their premises to make them accessible to people with physical or sensory disabilities.	☐	☐
Do you provide an information desk staffed by 'friendly faces'? Remember, first impressions count! People won't be encouraged to return if they are met by unhelpful members of staff.	☐	☐
Do you have staff who can speak some of the languages spoken by people in your local community and who understand the issues they face? This all helps to make learners from minority ethnic groups feel more comfortable.	☐	☐
Are you and your staff familiar with the Race Relations (Amendment) Act 2000, which details providers' responsibilities to offer equal opportunities to all staff and learners?	☐	☐
Do you provide an information, advice and guidance service? Learners need to know that the courses they are pursuing are *relevant*, and that the skills and qualifications they gain will be useful to them when seeking employment. They also need to know what opportunities are available to them for further progression.	☐	☐

Partnerships

If not doing so already, it is worth thinking about working in partnership with other organisations in your local community in order to meet the many varied needs that your learners may have.

There are many people and organisations in the community that can supply learning providers with valuable information about learners' needs, so check them out!

Here is an example of successful partnership working between a college of further education and the local community:

EETAC (the Employment, Education & Training Access Centre) is part of Leicester College and works in partnership with community providers. It offers

'Return to Learn' taster courses (for people aged 19+), e.g. 'Fun with Computers'.

> 'Our aim is to encourage those of you who have not taken part in education for some time. There are no qualifications attached to these courses, no pressure to pass, you just have fun learning something new.'

For those who wish to take their learning further, the centre also offers 'Skills Building Pathway', a programme that enables learners to gain accreditation. Subjects include computing, computing and basic English, maths, and dyslexia with IT.

The centre emphasises that learning is offered in a friendly, relaxed and fully supported environment with flexible hours of study.

	Yes	No
Do you already work with, or have you considered working with, community learning champions/mentors?	☐	☐
Are you in contact with representatives from local minority ethnic groups to find out what particular learning needs these groups may have?	☐	☐
Do you work with your local branch of Age Concern, the University of the Third Age or the WEA (Workers' Educational Association) to provide courses for older learners?	☐	☐
Have you thought about working with trade union learning representatives, local employers or advocacy groups?	☐	☐

3

Using ICT to widen participation

What does 'widening participation' mean?

What exactly is meant by the term 'widening participation'? The Learning and Skills Council offer the following definition:

> Widening participation is a process that tries to make education after the age of 16 more attractive and supportive to people who wouldn't usually take part in it. The learning might take place in the workplace, local community, online or at home.

> An important part of widening participation is making education and training programmes more appealing and suitable to a range of learners and circumstances. This is done with the support of a range of training providers including employers, colleges and local education authorities.
> Successful Participation for All: Widening Adult Participation Strategy
> Consultation (LSC 2004)

How can it be used?

So how can ICT be used in the process of widening participation? How can it be incorporated into education and training programmes to make them more appealing to a wider range of learners? Let's have a look at some strategies that could be used.

Taster sessions

Open days, taster sessions and short courses, e.g. 'Bite Size' introductory courses, can attract new learners. Such short, focused learning experiences offer people the opportunity to learn a little about topics before making any long-term commitment. Best of all, they are usually offered free of charge.

By helping people to see the relevance of learning to their lives, and to develop the confidence to learn, we can encourage their participation. Such sessions might be held on Saturdays or at the beginning of a college term or during an Adult Learners' Week.

Taster sessions are available in a wide variety of subjects to suit all interests and ages; for example:

> literacy or numeracy;
> ESOL (English for speakers of other languages);
> creative writing;
> foreign languages;
> television journalism;
> radio journalism;
> pottery;
> art;
> cookery;
> crafts;
> dance classes;
> fitness classes.

And of course, we mustn't forget ICT:

> *ICT is highly motivating and can attract people to return to learning.*
> A. Clarke, *Online Learning and Social Exclusion* (2002)

ICT can be used as a tool to motivate people to learn and can provide an added incentive when trying to attract and retain new learners. Many colleges and community centres offer taster sessions in all the main computer applications:

> word processing;
> spreadsheets;
> desktop publishing;
> presentation graphics;
> Internet and e-mail;
> database;
> web page design.

Anecdotal evidence also shows that ICT is a powerful motivator in encouraging adults to participate in basic skills courses. Literacy, numeracy and ESOL can all be combined with ICT to offer taster sessions – for example:

> Computing for skills for life;
> English with Computers;
> ESOL with Computing.

First Steps/short courses and accredited courses

After you have attracted learners to taster sessions and whetted their appetites to know more about a subject, you can then offer short, introductory courses in that subject. While these may not carry any accreditation, certificates of completion could be offered to signal the learners' achievement and give them further encouragement to continue with their learning.

As with taster sessions, short courses can be offered in a wide variety of subjects – for example:

> Computing for Absolute Beginners;
> Computing for the Terrified;

> Webwise – introduction to the Internet and e-mail;
> First Steps in Computing.

Many organisations also offer computing courses specifically aimed at groups in the community that may be classed as socially disadvantaged.

Older learners Research findings have shown that older learners tend to be more comfortable learning with their own peer group, and there has been an increase in the number and range of ICT classes catering specifically for the older learner, for example:

> Computing for the Over 50s;
> Computer Skills for the Over 55s;
> Computing for Older Learners.
> Classes specifically for those who are retired are often offered in partnership with local branches of Age Concern, the University of the Third Age (U3A) and the Workers' Educational Association (WEA).

However, not all older learners prefer to learn with their own age group. There are also examples of successful intergenerational learning in computing classes aimed at 'Fathers and Sons', or 'Grandparents and Grandchildren'.

As an example of how the young can pass their skills on to their elders, since November 2004, Age Concern Leicestershire and Rutland and Age Concern Oadby and Wigston have linked up with the Meadows Primary School in Wigston, Leicester, for a *'Teach your Granny/Granddad Scheme'*. The 10 year-old pupils are the tutors, teaching their grandparents IT skills with the help of laptops loaned from Age Concern. The grandparents then use their newly acquired IT skills to record their memories, e.g. of schooldays, daily life, the war, etc., and in this way contribute to their grandchildren's history project. Age Concern hopes eventually to roll out the project with other schools in the Leicester area.

Have you thought of working with a local school in this way to encourage intergenerational learning? Parents and grandparents could use their new-found computing skills to help children and grandchildren with their homework.

Women Running 'Women Only' groups is particularly useful when trying to attract learners from certain minority ethnic communities where, e.g. for religious reasons, women are usually taught separately from men. You might want to think about joining forces with your local branches of Age Concern or the WEA to provide locations for learning in the heart of various communities.

> Age Concern Newcastle began offering computer taster sessions at an Asian Women's lunch club in the city. When these sessions proved popular, regular weekly computer sessions were offered at the Age Concern centre itself. The women now go to the centre for these sessions, something that they wouldn't have done before.

> The WEA in Nottingham offers a free weekly computer workshop specifically for Asian women at a community centre in the St Ann's area of the city, a district with a high level of unemployment.

'I keep on learning more and more. Maybe in the future I can work with what I'm learning.' (a learner with the WEA's Community ICT Project)

WAITS (Women Acting in Today's Society) offers education and training opportunities to a number of different women's support groups. Many of the women who attend these groups would find it difficult for health or personal safety reasons to enter mainstream educational establishments.

WAITS (Women Acting in Today's Society), a charitable educational trust based in Edgbaston, Birmingham, offers education and training to socially excluded women of all ages, races and religions across the city of Birmingham and throughout the West Midlands. Using laptop computers, the organisation has taken learning out to the following women's groups:

> Sickle Cell and Thalassaemia Women's support group

> WINS (Women in Need of Support) – a support group for survivors of domestic violence

> Imaan – a Somalian Women's support group

> a Chinese women's support group

The organisation also offers one-to-one ICT training in women's own homes for those who have experienced domestic violence and are afraid to go out into the community to attend traditional educational institutions.

Offering classes in familiar locations such as primary schools and nurseries can also be very useful for attracting women learners with young children:

'I was introduced to this course through my daughter's nursery; the staff informed me that the computer course was especially designed for absolute beginners. I was a little apprehensive to join because I knew nothing about computers and found the whole idea a little daunting, but with a little encouragement and support from the staff I plucked up the courage to start the course. The nursery was a suitable and convenient place for me to do the course because it meant that my two year old son would be taken care of.' (female learner, Adult Education Ladywood & Perry Barr, Birmingham)

Learners with literacy or numeracy needs Many organisations experiment with different ways of delivering the basic skills of literacy and numeracy, often with the support of ICT. There is anecdotal evidence that ICT skills frequently have been developed as a byproduct of such courses. Courses are offered such as:

> Computing with Basic Skills;
> Basic Computer Skills with Key Skills;
> Computing for skills for life.

Another interesting way to use ICT to help adult learners with their reading and writing skills is to set up collaborative stories online. The tutor starts the story off, and then each learner reads what has gone before and adds a paragraph to the story. Such online stories are good fun and very motivating.

Learners with ESOL needs ICT can be used to support work with ESOL learners, e.g. by using interactive language programmes. There are many such programmes available on CD-ROM. Some colleges offer courses combining the two subjects, e.g.:

> ESOL and Beginners' Computing;
> English and Computers;
> Improve your English using a Computer.

Learners with learning difficulties

One organisation has used digital photography in its work with people who experience learning difficulties.

> The WEA in Leicester has run a digital photography course 'ITforMe.com' for students with learning difficulties. During the course the group progressed from basic IT to more sophisticated knowledge about the use of digital cameras and the way in which images can be used creatively with a computer.

Learners with disabilities With the evolution of adaptive technology, many organisations can now offer ICT facilities to adults with physical and sensory disabilities who in the past may have been excluded from such opportunities. Specially designed ICT equipment such as keyboards with larger keys, different types of mouse, larger screens, etc., can now help learners with a variety of disabilities.

Adaptive equipment being used by a visually impaired learner at the Bridge Centre, Hythe, Kent

Photograph courtesy of Mike Peek, Kent Association for the Blind

The organisation BASIC (Brain and Spinal Injury Charity), based in Salford, Manchester, offers computer training to people who have suffered brain injuries in order to help them back into employment.

BASIC is a support service for people who have a disability caused by an accident, brain haemorrhage, brain tumour or stroke. In partnership with the WEA and Salford University, BASIC's computer centre offers computer training and learndirect courses to clients aged 18–70. The centre is also researching and piloting memory training techniques to teach clients to touch-type by developing other memory pathways to replace those lost or damaged through brain injury. Such variety of training will help those who wish to get back into employment.

'I have been learning to word process for eight months. I began to do this because I had trouble turning our computer at home on and off. My two children would laugh at me. Now I feel much more confident, and not as intimidated by it because I have discovered that whatever you write you can correct before you print off your final copy. Before I had my car accident I was a nurse and of course a computer plays a large part in nursing these days, unlike when I trained back in 1976.' (female learner with BASIC)

Learners with mental health difficulties

The organisation Solent Mind, based in Southampton, has used ICT to help learners overcome problems of poor self-esteem and lack of confidence.

Solent Mind, purchased a number of wireless laptops with funding from the WON (Wireless Outreach Network) project managed by NIACE. The equipment is taken to locations in the county of Hampshire, e.g. to psychiatric hospitals, day hospitals and day centres for people with severe mental health difficulties, and is used for formal learning in literacy, language, numeracy and ICT as well as for informal instruction in accessing e-mails and searching the Internet. This has helped many learners regain confidence, and some have progressed to supporting other learners on a voluntary basis or even to their becoming tutors themselves.

The above are just a few of the socially disadvantaged groups that can be attracted to learning through the use of ICT.

Learners completing short courses and given the right encouragement, information and guidance may wish to progress on to longer courses with accreditation. The following appear to be the most popular accredited ICT courses:

> CLAIT (Computer Literacy and Information Technology), e.g. CLAIT Plus, CLAIT Level 2 or New CLAIT;

> ECDL (European Computer Driving Licence). This is an internationally recognised qualification intended to provide competence in computer skills. The key computer applications are all covered within the course, together with their practical use in the workplace and in society in general.

Using hobbies and interests as a 'hook'

There is much anecdotal evidence that ICT can be used as a 'hook' to draw people into learning, especially when coupled with their hobbies and interests.

For instance, tracing family histories has become a favourite hobby with many people. Many colleges of further education and other organisations have capitalised on this interest by offering short courses such as 'The Internet for Family Historians', focusing on useful websites for family historians. As a result of such courses, learners often want to know more about the various functions of a computer and go on to pursue other more formal and accredited ICT courses.

ICT can be used alongside traditional teaching and learning methods as part of a blended learning approach. PowerPoint slides and presentations, printed handouts using digital photos, CD-ROMs of material, etc., can all be used to enhance the teaching and learning experience in a variety of subjects. Digital photography is a great way to record learners' work and progress, especially in arts and crafts subjects. (See the section on **e-learning tools,** page 41.)

The following examples of popular hobbies/interests and activities for which ICT resources can be used may provide tutors with food for thought on how to use ICT to motivate learners and enhance the learning experience.

Jewellery making Digital cameras can be used in jewellery making classes.

> At the Swarthmore Centre, part of the Leeds Adult and Community Learning Service, students in a jewellery making class have been learning to use a digital camera to take photos of their work for display in online galleries or web albums for access by friends, family and potential clients. Digital photos of their paper designs and work are also being incorporated into the Visual Learning Records that form part of their portfolios. In addition, they have made short video clips of tutors demonstrating various jewellery-making techniques which will form part of a digital CD library. Learners will then be able to borrow the CDs to review what they have done or to catch up on missed classes.

Football One college capitalised on an interest in sport to attract new learners.

> Preston College, one of the participants in the NIACE-managed WIPE (Widening Participation and e-Learning) initiative, has developed and piloted a CD-ROM based on the history of football aimed at encouraging hard-to-reach groups to enter learning.

Gardening and garden design A rising number of adults want to know more about gardening, particularly organic gardening.

A free online organic gardening course is offered by the Greater Manchester Community Grid for Learning, part of the WEA in the North West of England.

Individual learners or community groups can log on to the 'Gardening Online' course whenever they want and wherever they have access to the Internet. The course covers a wide range of topics using interactive tutorials, fun exercises and instructions for outdoor work in the garden. To make the topics more interesting for learners, ICT authoring tools have been used to create a wildlife 'Webquest'.

Gardening tutors may wish to offer the course, or individual topics from it, as an 'extra' to classes they are already running.

The WEA in the North West has been running a free pilot project of the course on a VLE (Virtual Learning Environment) with an e-tutor. This format has the added benefits of feedback on assignments, discussion forums, news items, a photo gallery, chat facilities and useful resources. The WEA has been very pleased with the level of participation and interaction.

Take a look at the website **www.learners.org.uk** (go to Courses: Gardening Online).

'Learners can enjoy gardening when the weather's nice and do the online learning when the weather's at its worst.'

The Greater Manchester Community Grid for Learning runs a number of short online courses in a variety of subjects and is open to suggestions from individuals and community education providers for developing further courses – a good example of consulting the local community about learning needs.

Art You could use ICT in an art class to give an added dimension to a learner's work.

> Learners attending an art class run by the WEA in Leicester used ICT to add a new dimension to their work. As well as learning watercolour painting techniques and experimenting in drawing with pencil and charcoal, they learned how to scan their finished paintings/drawings and produce a digital image. The images were then used to create items such as personally designed greetings cards.

> To attract learners on to an accredited ICT course, the Bottesford Community College has combined ICT with an interest in art to offer a course in ECDL (European Computer Driving Licence) and Discovering Art.

Pottery Tutors working for Hull City Council's Adult Education Service have imported digital photographs into a PowerPoint presentation which they use as a teaching/learning aid in their life drawing and pottery classes. Handouts are also produced containing information about materials required, methods used and suggestions for further study.

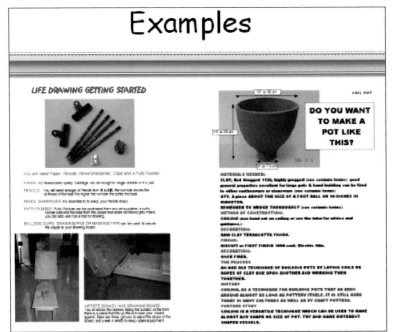

23

Local and family history Current interest in local history and family history is proving to be a very successful 'hook' to engage adults in First Steps learning. Many people now use computer programs to write up their family histories and create family trees.

There is a plethora of websites to search for information on local and family history; see **http://www.cyndislist.com** for a list of genealogy websites on the Internet.

Here's a fun way for all members of the family to take part in a learning experience.

As part of NIACE's TrEACL (Technology to Enhance Adult and Community Learning) initiative, one enterprising LEA has collaborated with adult learners and tutors taking part in its family learning programme to develop a project that promotes and develops the use of e-learning.

To engage adults and their children with e-learning for the first time, a learning programme called the *History Detective* has been developed, consisting of a mixture of offline and electronic activities designed to appeal to all age groups. An interactive CD of the course materials, called *How to be a History Detective*, encourages learners to research information using the Internet and uses quizzes for learners to check what they have learned.

HOW TO BE A HISTORY DETECTIVE

Hello,
and

1
2
3
4
5
6
7

So you want to be a History Detective? Well here's where you start ...
During your stay at the Academy, the Chief Detective will help you to learn history detective skills.

This CD will help you to practice those skills, so that you can use them in a 'real' investigation, and record your findings along the way.

You can also check what you have learned in a fun quiz and award yourself a golden acorn.

New detectives will need to learn how to use this CD, so Click **Help**.

Learning languages We have already mentioned that interactive computer programmes can be a very useful aid for ESOL learners. Such interactive programmes are equally useful for learners of other languages.

Knowsley Metropolitan Borough Council produced a '*Revise your Spanish*' CD with funding from NIACE's TrEACL (Technology to Enhance Adult and Community Learning) initiative, to help students revise what they had learned in class as part of a blended learning strategy. This multimedia programme was designed to meet the needs of disadvantaged learners and addresses basic skills, ICT and study skills. It's a fun way for young and old alike to practise their language skills by looking at everyday situations and using games to reinforce the learning.

Fitness classes Digital cameras can be used in fitness classes.

A yoga tutor working for Portsmouth City Council's Wymering Centre has produced a teaching and learning aid by taking digital photos of her students. The photos show various yoga positions and give their correct technical names and advice on how to attain the position. The photographs have been imported into a PowerPoint presentation which learners can then use in order to practise the positions between classes or catch up on classes that were missed. Photographs of the learners can also help them to see how far they have progressed during the course.

25

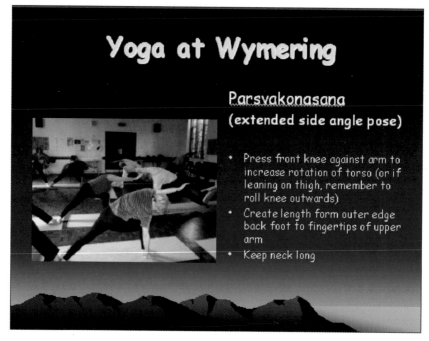

Many other hobbies and interests can be combined with ICT to enhance the learning experience. For example, digital cameras, scanners and PowerPoint presentations can be used in the following activities:

> Recipes and cookery demonstrations can be illustrated using digital photographs, and online cookery books can be produced for cookery classes. These could also be used in language classes so that learners can translate their favourite recipes.

> Flower arranging

> Designing and making greetings cards

> Knitting/sewing patterns

> Interior design

> Designing logos for T-shirts, place mats, etc.

> Learning to play a musical instrument. The company Gigajam produces software enabling a learner to gain ICT skills while

learning to play a musical instrument: visit
http://www.gigajam.com

> Materials to support learning English

- *Scrabble* – e-scrabble is an easy and enjoyable way for anyone studying English, ESOL or even basic skills to learn and use new vocabulary. You can even play scrabble in a foreign language – visit **http://www.scrabble.com**

- *Crossword solving online* – tutors can create their own crosswords to include in classes – take a look at **http://www.shophub.com/crossword.cfm**

The list of hobbies, interests and activities that can be supported by ICT is practically endless. Have a go – see what else you can think of!

ICT mentors

Mentoring is an increasingly popular concept in today's world, and mentors provide a much needed support system in businesses, schools and other educational institutions.

> *To help and support people to manage their own learning in order to maximise their potential, develop their skills, improve their performance, and become the person they want to be.*
> E. Parsloe, *Coaching, Mentoring and Assessing* (1992)

Mentors are not necessarily experts in their field but are people with an interest and certain level of competence in their chosen subject who wish to share their knowledge, skills and experience with others. They may be retired or unemployed people with some spare time on their hands, or volunteers from the local community representing a religious or ethnic group.

Many community and voluntary organisations use the services of volunteer helpers in their learning programmes, especially in ICT. Such volunteers may be known as ICT mentors, ICT volunteers, ICT supporters, Computer Buddies, Internet Angels or Community Learning Champions.

27

Whatever title they are known by, these volunteers fulfil a vital role in many classes. Without their assistance, many voluntary and community organisations would not be able to offer the range of ICT training courses that they do – or, indeed, to offer ICT training at all.

There are enormous benefits to volunteers in their role:

'Volunteering has really given me a sense of well-being and satisfaction in the knowledge that I am able to help expand people's knowledge a little bit. I recommend it to anybody. I have been asked to tutor classes for the WEA and I have also been offered some teaching hours at the local college – all from volunteering! So much for my retirement!' (volunteer with the WEA in Mansfield)

A mentor can help learners to:

> raise their achievement;
> develop their personal and social skills;
> raise their self-confidence;
> build their self-esteem.

Raising self-confidence and self-esteem is particularly important for adults who are returning to learning after a long gap in their studies, especially if they have negative memories of their school days and have not taken part in any learning/training courses since then. They need to be motivated to learn, and mentors can prove to be of great benefit here.

There is much anecdotal evidence from organisations of mentors who have proved very effective in helping learners with a variety of needs and interests, ranging from those with literacy, language or numeracy requirements to older people, women's groups and people with learning difficulties and/or disabilities or those with mental health problems.

Many organisations running mentoring programmes have found that such programmes help to retain learners and improve their results.

Photograph courtesy of Philip Birch, Training Highway, Kent

Training Highway, a computer and Internet training company based in Kent, provides ICT training throughout the county, mainly to older learners. Their ICT mentors, known as 'Highway Helpers', help with classes held in a variety of locations, from community centres, village halls and clubs to residential care homes, schools, people's own homes and centres for the retired.

Outreach: the importance of choosing the right venue

Providing learning sessions in venues that people are familiar and comfortable with will appeal to those who wouldn't normally think of going into a formal learning environment such as a college of further education.

Outreach work is a well researched area:

> *There is widespread recognition among adult education*
> *researchers, analysts and practitioners that outreach work is one*
> *of the most effective ways of attracting new and different learners,*
> *especially those who are the most socially excluded.*
> V. McGivney, *Spreading the Word: Reaching out to New Learners*

Why not think about running ICT sessions in local libraries, village halls, church halls, faith centres, working men's clubs, pubs, shopping centres or primary schools? Most people will be familiar with one or more of these locations, and for the most disadvantaged or poorest people 'local' means very close to where they live.

UK Online, learndirect centres and the People's Network

The government has invested significantly in ICT over recent years in an attempt to address skills shortages in the workforce. In April 2005 there were some 6000 UK Online and 2400 learndirect centres throughout the country offering learners a flexible way of learning. Recent statistics show that 99 per cent of UK households are within 10 km of a learndirect or UK Online centre, and 89 per cent are within walking distance (3 km) (DfES 2005).

Half of the UK Online centres are in public libraries, and the People's Network has ensured that 92 per cent of public libraries offer free Internet access. Many libraries offer Internet taster sessions and other special IT sessions. Some, working in partnership with local colleges or adult education centres, are able to offer basic computing and CLAIT courses. Leicestershire libraries offer such sessions as:

> Gardening on the Net;
> Scanners in Action;
> Galleries on the Net;

> Choose a Good Read on the Net;
> Coffee, Chat and Computers;
> e-mail: How to Set Up an Account.

Other UK Online centres are located in libraries, Internet cafés, shopping malls, football grounds, community centres and village halls. Such local and familiar locations may appeal to learners who would not be inclined to enter a formal educational establishment.

One adult education college has tutors working in public libraries across the city. Leicester Adult Education College works in partnership with Leicester City Library Services to offer free ICT courses at the UK Online centre next to the main library in Leicester, plus outreach locations across the city. The college's outreach programme includes Beginners' Workshops, Designing a T-Shirt, Beginners' Guides to Computing, Internet Introduction courses, WebWise and a variety of taster sessions.

Findings from work in e-learning centres

> Learners have more ways to learn. They can use a mixture of computers and the Internet, CD-ROMs, videotapes and workbooks for their courses. Some of these exercises take just 15 minutes, while others take several hours but are usually broken down into 'bite-sized chunks' of learning. Over 500 online courses are on offer from learndirect in ICT, basic skills, and general and specialist business and management. The courses range from beginner to advanced levels, with many leading to qualifications. Basic skills courses are free and many others are subsidised by the government.
> Learning is more flexible. Learners can study at a learndirect centre or, if they have Internet access, at home or at work. Such flexible study arrangements mean that they can fit learning around their work and family commitments and can learn what they want, where they want and when they want.

> Since 2000, 1.7 million learners have studied with learndirect and almost one third of these had not taken part in any learning in the previous three years. Many of these learners are from the 2000 most deprived and geographically disadvantaged communities in England, and 80 per cent are from key disadvantaged target groups, i.e. people with literacy and numeracy needs, the unemployed, the disabled, single parents, the over 65s and people from minority ethnic groups (see National Audit Office 2005).

Portable ICT equipment

The advent of portable ICT equipment such as laptop computers has made it possible for a wide variety of venues to be used that wouldn't previously have been considered. (See pages 39–40 for a fuller picture of the types of venue used.)

Here's an example of an enterprising organisation making use of community venues for their ICT programmes, including the field where a village hall gala was being held.

The United Villages Partnership (UVP) operates in an area of ex-mining villages around Barnsley, Yorkshire, where there is a low level of learning participation – only 37.5 per cent of households say they access the Internet. Using wireless laptop equipment, UVP can go out into the community to talk to prospective learners about what is on offer in terms of the Internet and other ICT programmes. While some sessions are held at the UVP centre, known as the 'Surf Shack', in the Mapplewell and Staincross Village Hall, they also have outreach venues in a local Methodist church and a working men's club and regularly visit the local Co-op store to talk to learners. When the Village Hall recently celebrated its second anniversary with a gala, wireless laptops were used in the middle of a field to demonstrate the type of provision that UVP can offer.

Using wireless laptops at Mapplewell and Staincross Village Hall Gala
Photograph courtesy of June Oates, UPV Learning Centre Network

Some projects combining portable ICT equipment and Outreach

Wireless Outreach Network (WON)

In 2003 the DfES provided funding for a three-year laptop initiative using networks of wireless laptops for increasing access to learning through technology for socially and economically disadvantaged adults in England. This became known as the Wireless Outreach Network (WON) initiative. A total of 269 organisations were successful in their bids for funding.

Regular monitoring surveys have revealed much useful information about the groups of learners using the equipment, the venues where the equipment is being used and how it is being used.

Which socially disadvantaged groups do we mean? The best outreach work concentrates on those with the least chances, such as:

> asylum seekers and refugees;
> black and minority ethnic groups;
> women returners;
> visually impaired learners;
> people with physical, learning or mental health disabilities;
> victims of domestic violence;
> residents in warden-aided complexes;
> travellers;
> lone parents;
> prostitutes wishing to change their lives;
> farmers' co-operatives;
> homeless people;
> carers;
> young unemployed;
> older people.

Henshaw's Society for Blind People, based in Manchester and Liverpool, purchased 12 wireless laptops with its WON funding. With these the Society offers 'Skillstep', a number of learning courses tailored to help visually impaired adults gain the skills they need to find employment. The courses are provided free of charge, and learners receive training in word processing, the Internet and email.

The Skillstep project co-ordinator worked with one of the Skillstep trainees to prepare a PowerPoint presentation that also made use of the voice facility on the laptop. The presentation focused on learners talking about their experiences on Skillstep courses.

Henshaw's has a good attendance rate at both its centres and a high retention rate on its courses. A good percentage of learners on the Skillstep programme progress into paid employment or voluntary work.

One WON beneficiary reached out to the over 50s, particularly members of minority ethnic communities.

> Age Concern Newcastle purchased 16 laptops with its WON funding. The laptops are being used by various non-ICT classes; for example, the writers' group uses the Internet to access information on writers, the craft group looks up craft sites and the artists' group looks up information on painters and art galleries together with information regarding exhibition sites in the area.
>
> The laptops are also used to attract new learners from members of minority ethnic communities in the Newcastle area, for example older members of the local Chinese community.
>
> Finally, the laptops have been taken to an Asian women's lunch club, where they have been used for taster sessions in word processing, e-mail and searching the Internet for sites of interest, e.g. Asian newspaper websites. Many of these women now attend regular weekly computer sessions at the Age Concern centre.

Venues The list of venues that could be used in the community with wireless laptop equipment is endless. Think about it – no more trailing wires for tutor or learner to trip over! That's surely a great advantage of using such equipment. Examples of such venues include:

> hospital wards and therapy rooms;
> community centres;
> schools – many have dedicated community rooms for use by parents;
> day centres;
> care homes;
> people's own homes;
> village and parish halls;
> faith centres;

> working men's clubs;
> local libraries;
> sheltered accommodation;
> farms;
> pubs;
> theatre foyers;
> hostels for the homeless, victims of domestic violence, etc.

What were the laptops used for? In addition to taster sessions and formal courses in all the main computer applications, the laptops were used in a wide range of activities, including:

> literacy, language and numeracy;
> design work (e.g. T-shirt logos or placemats; posters and leaflets for community organisations);
> job searches;
> study/course work;
> confidence building;
> information and guidance;
> staff development programmes;
> reminiscence work with older learners, e.g. typing up life histories;
> family learning (e.g. fathers' ICT beginners' courses with their children acting as mentors);
> music technology;
> digital photography;
> website creation.

Impact Because of their portability, (wireless) laptop computers are ideal for outreach locations with which people are familiar and feel comfortable. This is especially helpful for those who are taking their first steps back into learning.

Here are some of the providers' findings regarding the impact of using portable technology for reaching learners from socially and economically disadvantaged groups:

'The wireless technology has enabled us to deliver a wider range of learning opportunities through various venues within the community, thereby engaging people who would not participate in learning through a college.'

'The WON project has enabled our college to expand our use of IT in widening participation in two ways: by increasing motivation to learn through the use of IT, and by extending the curriculum offered to marginalised groups who experience access barriers (either transport or confidence) to current main provision.'

'Being able to lend laptops to disadvantaged young people has helped them gain an interest in their own personal development, which has subsequently led to their engaging in a variety of community work and activities, and has assisted in helping them to gain employment or start a business.'

'Wireless technology provides learners with a non-traditional method of learning which has stimulated their interest and enthusiasm.'

A selection of case studies from the project can be found on the NIACE website: see **www.niace.org.uk/Research/ICT/WON.htm**

Wireless laptops being used in a class for learners with literacy and/or numeracy needs at Birmingham Rathbone Society

Photograph by Jackie Essom, NIACE

Widening Participation and e-learning (WIPE)

The WIPE project, launched in October 2004 and managed by NIACE, was part of the Learning and Skills Council's programme to promote the use of e-learning in adult and community learning. Twelve organisations were funded to initiate and manage innovative e-learning action research projects in the context of widening participation for socially disadvantaged groups. Many of the organisations made extensive use of portable ICT equipment within their projects.

The project's intended outcomes were:

> to produce new knowledge and practical theories in the effective use of e-learning and ICT;

> to open up learning in terms of delivery and content to hard-to-reach learners;

> to identify staff development needs in the use of technology to support teaching and learning.

Target groups involved in the project included:

> homeless young people recovering from drug or alcohol dependency;
> young people with mild to moderate learning difficulties;
> young unemployed mothers;
> single parents;
> visually impaired learners;
> employees of small and medium sized businesses, including those who are unskilled or semi-skilled;
> learners living in rural areas;
> older learners, including those with long-term mental health difficulties.

The Bolton LEA and Bolton Community College worked in partnership with a local day centre to widen participation for adult learners with long-term mental health difficulties.

Bolton LEA and Bolton Community College targeted learners with enduring mental health difficulties who attend St George's day centre in Bolton. Laptops and a data projector were purchased with the WIPE funding. The projector was used to demonstrate the possibilities that computers could offer. For example, strategy games were demonstrated to engage learners' interest and to encourage them to use the laptops.

The computing sessions were delivered at the day centre by a tutor who himself had experienced mental health problems and could empathise with the problems faced by the learners. Ongoing progress was noted in a reflective journal, and Bolton Community College plans to use the findings to inform its future plans regarding e-learning.

Learners using portable ICT equipment at St George's Day Centre, Bolton
Photograph courtesy of Liz Foster, Staff Development Manager, Bolton Community College

A variety of e-learning and ICT approaches were tried out in the WIPE project, including:

> using digital cameras in non-ICT classes;

> using interactive online learning materials for literacy;

> using digital video technology to improve the teaching and learning of life skills;

> developing a website to provide information and advice;

> using enabling technology for visually impaired learners;

> using strategy games to engage the interest of learners;

> developing and piloting a new CD-ROM based on the history of football.

This section has given just a brief idea of how e-learning and ICT can be used to engage learners from socially and economically disadvantaged groups.

Fuller descriptions of all the WIPE projects and the final project report can be found on the NIACE website:

40

www.niace.org.uk/Research/ICT/WIPE.htm

4

e-learning tools and activities for engaging new learners

e-learning tools

In addition to the more obvious ICT equipment such as desktop PCs and laptop computers, you might want to consider using some of the following e-learning tools to enhance your teaching/training sessions.

Data projectors and screens

A data projector can be used to:

> project the view of a computer screen on to a large screen for the whole class to see;

> display learning materials to a whole group, e.g. exercises and quizzes;

> show presentations to a group using an application such as PowerPoint.

Digital cameras

Digital cameras are useful for photographing activities to be printed, published or placed on the web. They provide:

> an instant record of an activity which can be used to stimulate further discussion and learner interaction;

> a record of events and work in progress which learners can use to create visual diaries and portfolios;

> a showcase for art and design work by tutors and/or learners;
> illustrations for cookery, pottery, fitness and other classes;
> a means of creating photo stories, which could be used to stimulate conversation in language classes.

Many digital cameras will also take short video clips of about 30 seconds' duration. These can be used to illustrate techniques or to record acquired skills in such areas as sport, fitness, design and crafts.

Here's how a group of older learners used ICT equipment to create a novel tribute to their city and its heritage.

At Age Concern Newcastle, wireless laptops and a digital camera were used by learners to create the 'Geordie Bayeux tapestry'. The tapestry is made up of photographs of the city of Newcastle and formed part of an exhibition in 2003. There have since been requests to turn some of the images in the tapestry into postcards.

A multimedia mobile phone could be useful in outreach situations where photographs can be taken and sent back to base.

Other equipment might include:

> CDs of interactive learning materials, e.g. for language courses;
> DVDs;
> camcorders;
> interactive white boards;
> scanners;
> webcams.

Learners pursuing courses through Hull City Council's adult education service where e-learning tools such as digital cameras have been used have said:

'I feel that using the technology to record my work has added value to the course' (Dressmaking and tailoring class)

'Having colour printouts of the model means I can continue to work on the portrait at home' (Portrait and costume class)

'I love being able to have copies of my work!' (Drawing and painting class)

'Hot Potatoes'

This is an authoring tool that allows tutors to develop:

> online quizzes and exercises;
> crosswords;
> other web-based interactive learning modules.

The program generates web pages which can be saved and used on any computer. For further information, see
http://www.halfbakedsoftware.com

e-learning activities

Tutors/trainers may wish to think about incorporating some of the following activities into their teaching/training sessions using e-learning software.

Quizzes

These can be very useful resources to use in learning:

> they can be fun:

> they can be engaging – learners can develop the questions themselves;

> they can be used in almost all subjects;

> they can provide an initial means of assessment;

> they can be conducted at a distance, e.g. quizzes between college teams, pub teams, etc.;

> they can be helpful for revision;

> they can be used to encourage group interaction;

> they can help in the reinforcement and checking of new learning points.

Games

Using computer games in learning sessions can:

> engage younger and older learners alike, so is very useful for inter-generational learning;

> motivate learners and reinforce new learning points;

> give instant and visual feedback on the learner's performance.

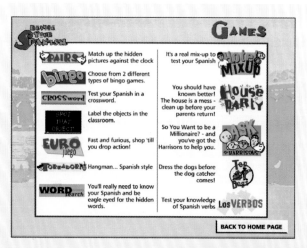

This web page gives some examples of interactive games from the *Revise your Spanish* CD, produced by Knowsley Metropolitan Borough Council. Such games aid revision and reinforcement of language learning in an enjoyable way for all the family.

Online simulations

Many websites provide access to online simulations which can prepare learners for the world of work. The interactive website http://www.moneymatterstome.co.uk helps learners to understand day to day financial matters, e.g. when starting a new job or planning for retirement. It offers a series of interactive workshops, including a simulation of a cash machine.

Weblogs or blogs

These are non-commercial websites that use a dated diary or log format which is updated frequently with new information. They may provide links to articles, books and other websites which might be useful for learners preparing for assignments and discussions on various subjects, or providing resources for webquests.

Webquests

This is a flexible and powerful tool to aid learning that can be used with individuals or small groups. Webquests usually take the form of:

> scenarios – providing the background to the quest;
> tasks – outlining the aims and objectives of the quest;
> recommended resources – giving a list of online resources that provide all the information required to fulfil the webquest.

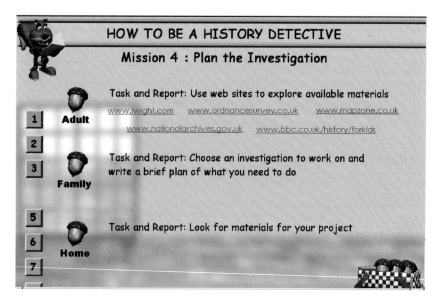

Example of a webquest from the How to be a History Detective CD

5

Summary

We hope that this guide has given you plenty of hints and tips on how to use ICT to engage, motivate and widen participation among socially disadvantaged groups.

As an *aide memoire* here is a summary of some good practice ideas to bear in mind when trying to attract and retain learners from these groups.

Accessibility Ensure that you are familiar with the Disability Discrimination Act and that premises (including outreach locations) are accessible to people with physical and/or sensory difficulties.

Community locations/outreach Taking learning opportunities out into the community using local and familiar venues is a key factor in reaching non-traditional learners and will often attract those who would not normally think of entering a more formal educational setting. Make the most of any outreach services that your organisation offers.

e-learning tools and activities Think about using e-learning tools and activities such as electronically produced handouts, digital photographs, CD-ROMs and video clips as part of a blended learning approach to enhance teaching and learning for both tutor and learner. The more interesting and varied the teaching session is, the more likely that learners will be motivated to continue their learning rather than dropping out.

• **Embedding** Consider embedding ICT into other activities such as literacy, numeracy and ESOL. In turn, these combined activities can be embedded into other subjects.

Flexibility Focus on creating your curriculum around your learners' interests and try to design learning sessions around your learners' needs. Is it possible to provide workshop sessions in the evenings or on Saturday mornings to attract those who cannot attend on a regular basis? Are crèche facilities available so that parents with young children can take part in learning sessions?

Hobbies/interests Capitalise on the hobbies and interests of your target group and use them as a 'hook' to attract people into First Steps learning.

Mentors Consider running a mentoring programme within your organisation. Mentors can provide a valuable resource to complement your teaching staff and enhance the services offered by your organisation. They can improve success rates and make a valuable contribution towards retaining learners.

Partnerships Liaise with representatives from local organisations and community groups to discover the learning needs of disadvantaged groups within your area. Such partners may also be able to provide you with suitable premises for outreach work that would be more familiar and comfortable for your target groups.

Portable ICT equipment Portable computer equipment such as laptop computers and wireless laptops can be used almost anywhere. If laptop batteries are fully charged, they even allow for taster events and learning sessions to take place where there is no electricity supply. New learners tend to find laptop computers less daunting to use than desktop computers. Best of all, using wireless laptops means no more trailing wires for tutors or students to trip over, so fewer worries over health and safety issues when using outreach locations.

Relevance Adults are more likely to be motivated to learn when they can see that the learning is not only interesting but also useful, and relevant to their lives. A good information, advice and guidance service can advise learners on how skills and qualifications will be useful to them when seeking employment and can also advise on further education opportunities.

Taster sessions/short courses Short, taster sessions in various subjects are helpful to potential learners and encourage their progression on to other courses. If possible, try running taster sessions in some familiar but non-traditional locations, e.g. shopping malls, libraries, hostels, village halls, pubs. A certificate of completion can be offered to show learners what they have achieved and give them encouragement to continue with their learning.

Welcoming environment Last, but by no means least, try to ensure that learners receive a warm and friendly welcome from your reception/information desk. A friendly and helpful service will mean a lot to learners, particularly those returning to learning after a long break.

6

Useful websites

http://www.abilitynet.org.uk – advice on accessibility for learners with disabilities (accessed 2 May 2006).

http://aceuk.blogspot.com – adult and community e-learning UK: a blog site written by an IT tutor containing free IT resources and e-learning news and reviews for the adult and community learning sector (accessed 2 May 2006).

http://www.aclearn.net – website containing electronic learning materials for use in FE and ACL (accessed 2 May 2006).

http://www.eldis.org/education/toolsresources.htm – a directory of online tools and resources for education (accessed 2 May 2006).

http://www.helpisathand.gov.uk – resources for UK Online centres, voluntary and community sector centres, public libraries, colleges, and adult and community learning centres (accessed 2 May 2006).

http://www.learndirect.co.uk – website containing details of all learndirect centres and online courses offered (accessed 2 May 2006).

http://www.nln.ac.uk/materials – a collection of learning objects for organisations and tutors dealing with post-16 learners (accessed 2 May 2006).

http://www.socialexclusionunit.gov.uk – a brief guide to the subject of social exclusion together with copies of reports produced by the unit (accessed 2 May 2006).

http://www.techdis,ac.uk – help for disabled learners and staff in using technology (accessed 2 May 2006).

http://ucl.ac.uk/learningtechnology/caa/hotpot – examples of 'Hot Potatoes' tools for creating interactive web-based activities for self-assessment purposes (accessed 2 May 2006).

http://www.ufi.com/UKOL – website containing details about UK Online centres, set up by the DfES to provide computer access to people in the community (accessed 2 May 2006).

http://www.vts.rdn.ac.uk/teachers – resources for teachers and trainers, e.g. free tutorials on using the Internet, worksheets and teaching support materials (accessed 2 May 2006).

7
Further reading

Clarke, A. (2002) *Online Learning and Social Exclusion*, Leicester: NIACE.

Clarke, A. and Hesse, C. (2004) *Online resources in the classroom: Using the World Wide Web to Deliver and Support Adult Learning*, Leicester: NIACE.

Clarke, A., Reeve, A., Essom, J., Scott, J., Aldridge, F. and Lindsay, K. (2003) *Adult and Community Learning Laptop Initiative Evaluation*, Leicester: NIACE.

DfES (2003) *The Skills for Life Survey: A National Needs and Impact Survey of Literacy, Numeracy and ICT Skills*, DfES Research Report 490, London: Her Majesty's Stationery Office.

DfES (2003) *21st Century Skills: Realising Our Potential*, the Skills Strategy White Paper, Her Majesty's Stationery Office, Cm. 5810, London: DfES.

DfES (2005) *Harnessing Technology: Transforming Learning and Children's Services*, London: DfES.

Essom, J. (2003) *ICT Mentors: A Support Skills Resource for Volunteers and Programme Co-ordinators in Community and Voluntary Organisations*, Leicester: NIACE.

Essom, J. (2004) *Widening the World with Wireless Laptops: The Impact of the Wireless Outreach Network Initiative on the Community*, Leicester: NIACE

Hardcastle, P. (2004) *Digital Cameras in Teaching and Learning*, Leicester: NIACE.

Kennedy, H. (1997) *Learning Works: Widening Participation in Further Education*, London: Further Education Funding Council (FEFC).

LSC (2004) *Successful Participation for All: Widening Adult Participation Strategy Consultation* London: LSC.

McGivney, V. (2002) *Spreading the Word: Reaching Out to New Learners*, Lifelines in Adult Learning No. 2, Leicester: NIACE.

National Audit Office (2005) *Extending Access to Learning through Technology: Ufi and the Learndirect Service*, London: The Stationery Office.

Owen, G. and Iqbal, K. (2004) *e-learning in Outreach*, Lifelines in Adult Learning No. 4, Leicester: NIACE.

Parsloe, E. (1992) *Coaching, Mentoring and Assessing*, London: Kogan Page.

Social Exclusion Unit (2004) *Breaking the Cycle: Taking Stock of Progress and Priorities for the Future*, London: ODPM Publications.

Social Exclusion Unit (2005) *Inclusion through Innovation: Tackling Social Exclusion through New Technologies*, London: ODPM Publications.

8

Glossary

ACL	adult and community learning
blended learning	the integration of conventional approaches with e-learning to gain the maximum benefits from both
DfES	Department for Education and Skills
e-learning	the use of technology to enhance the teaching and learning process
ESOL	English for speakers of other languages
ICT	information and communication technologies
LSC	Learning and Skills Council
multimedia	the integration of different presentation formats, e.g. video, audio, text, graphics, etc.
NIACE	National Institute of Adult Continuing Education
Online learning	learning with the help of information and communication technologies that requires a connection to the Internet.
TrEACL	Technology to Enhance Adult and Community Learning; a NIACE-managed project that has supported the development of a wide range of innovative e-learning projects, many of which have created new and interactive learning material
weblog	also known as a **blog**: a personal or non-commercial website that uses a dated diary or log format that is frequently updated with new information

WIPE   Widening Participation and e-Learning: an
action research project managed by NIACE
exploring e-learning in the context of widening
participation for 'hard-to-reach' learners

WON   Wireless Outreach Network: a NIACE-managed
project that provided the funding for networks
of wireless laptops to be used in widening
participation for socially disadvantaged groups
of learners.

>> More **e-guidelines** from **ⓝiace**

Guidance and support, accessible advice and useful examples of good practice for adult learning practitioners who want to use digital technology in all its forms to attract and support adult learners.

NEW

e-guidelines 5

e-learning and modern foreign language teaching

Jacky Elliott

ISBN 1 86201 229 6, January 2006, 56pp, £9.95, US$ 20.00, €17.00

The key practices and benefits of using e-learning to teach languages to adults explained.

The author illustrates blended learning – a mix of e-learning and traditional classroom methods. She looks at how e-learning can provide appropriate self-directed learning resources for adults, and examines task-based and topic-based learning, giving usable and adaptable examples of lessons and materials.

NEW

e-guidelines 6

Integrating ICT Skill for Life with financial education

Alan Clarke

ISBN 1 86201 275 X, March 2006, approx 48pp, £9.95, US$ 20.00, €

One of the appeals of the ICT Skill for Life standard is its potential for integration within other subjects ICT skills can thus be learned indirectly.

This guide provides a range of ideas, exercises and suggestions for integrating ICT with financial education, to the benefit of both subjects.

>>> More **e-guidelines** from NIACE

NEW

e-guidelines 8

e-learning for teaching English for Speakers of Other Languages

Mary Moss and Sue Southwood

ISBN 1 86201 228 8, March 2006, approx 48pp, £9.95, US$ 20.00, €17.00

A practical guide to help teachers of English for Speakers of Other Languages (ESOL) with the introduction of e-learning into their classes. Without technical jargon, and without assuming technical expertise, it covers the use of equipment, the creation of learning materials and ideas for teaching and learning activities.

It includes descriptions of the use of computers and technology such as interactive whiteboards and digital cameras, and puts forward practical ideas to use technology as a way of enhancing the quality of teaching and learning inside and outside the classroom.

NEW

e-guidelines 9

Supporting adult learners with dyslexia: harnessing the power of technology

Sally McKeown

ISBN: 1 86201 293 8, June 2006, 50pp, £9.95, US $20.00, €17.00

Information and guidance for tutors in any subject area who want to offer good-quality support for dyslexic learners.

Many people with dyslexia have found that the computer actually opens doors to learning and can help them minimise, if not overcome, their problems with text.

SPECIAL OFFER
Buy three or more e-guidelines for £7.00 each
€12.50
US $14.50 each

>>> More **e-guidelines** from NIACE

e-guidelines 1
Online resources in the classroom
Using the World Wide Web to deliver and support adult learning
Alan Clarke and Claudia Hesse
ISBN 1 86201 224 5, 2005, 60pp, £9.95, US$20.00, €17.00

Invaluable for tutors of any subject who need or want to use online resources in a face-to-face context.

e-guidelines 2
Digital cameras in teaching and learning
Phil Hardcastle
ISBN 1 86201 225 3, 2005, 36pp, £9.95, US$20.00, €17.00

Sets the use of digital cameras into current thinking about learning styles, provides many examples of good practice, and explores how they can help make learning more effective.

e-guidelines 3
Developing e-learning materials
Applying user-centred design
Shubhanna Hussain
ISBN 1 86201 226 1, 2005, 48pp, £9.95, US$20.00, €17.00

Explains the best ways to design and perfect your own e-learning resources. Applicable to all subject areas, and written specifically for those from a non-technical background.

e-guidelines 4
e-learning in outreach
Glyn Owen and Khawar Iqbal
ISBN 1 86201 227 X, 2005, 56pp, £9.95, US$20.00, €17.00

Covers all aspects of teaching, learning, the management of learning and the use of technology in an outreach context, providing information, guidance and support for practitioners in the community.

'Extremely successful at covering every aspect'

(e-learning age, April 2005)